The
Backwaters
Press

THE BACKWATERS PRIZE IN POETRY

LIVING
ROOM

Laura Bylenok

THE BACKWATERS PRESS · *An imprint of the University of Nebraska Press*

Decorative illustrations: "Árbol, Fase i," "Árbol,
Fase ii," "Árbol, Fase iii," "Árbol, Fase iv," and
"Árbol, Fase v" by Israel Aguilar Pacheco.

Library of Congress Cataloging-in-Publication Data
Names: Bylenok, Laura, 1982– author.
Title: Living room / Laura Bylenok.
Description: Lincoln: The Backwaters Press, an
      imprint of the University of Nebraska Press,
      [2022] | Series: The Backwaters Prize in Poetry |
      Winner of the 2021 Backwaters Prize in
      Poetry. | Includes bibliographical references.
Identifiers: LCCN 2022013284
ISBN 9781496232366 (paperback)
ISBN 9781496234599 (epub)
ISBN 9781496234605 (pdf)
Subjects: BISAC: POETRY / American /
      General | LCGFT: Poetry.
Classification: LCC PS3602.Y47 L58 2022 |
      DDC 811/.6—dc23/eng/20220321
LC record available at
      https://lccn.loc.gov/2022013284

Set in Garamond Premier by Mikala R. Kolander.
Designed by N. Putens.

The individual denoted by 'I' is not constituted merely by a body or a personal ego or consciousness. I am, of course, partially constituted by these immediate physical and mental structures, but I am also constituted by my ecological relations with the elements of my environment—relations in the image of which the structures of my body and consciousness are built.

—FREYA MATHEWS

We are all lichens.

—S. F. GILBERT

CONTENTS

LIVING ROOM

Autotheory

The problem is everything
is human. Where to go from there?

I say I
don't feel like myself.

I ate a little typhoid once, and the people there
instructed me without saying *okay, vomit!*

And no amount of listening
can generate knowledge of this kind.

I am, for example, eukaryote
before I am listening.

Mother, I
am listening for your instructions.

There's a little window in my room
with bars set into the concrete sill

to keep the things inside in
and outside out

and just now the translucent polyester curtain
baby blue as an old eyelid

waves in and out
and waves in

some cumbia from a car stereo
and then a horn, then almost gone

before I recognize it, a gesture in the air
of antiseptic.

Waiting Room

In the waiting room the TV goes static to snow. Nobody cares
or bothers to turn it down. It's not that I don't want to watch it.
Anything watched long enough can become something else, after
all, snow in a forest of light,

a zootrophic membrane backlighting the pines of a fragmented
and whole and vibrating forest

real neurons can't discern.

Zootrophic, adjective. Pertaining to the nourishment of animals.
From *zoo-*, animal, and *-trophic*, food. Because even a screen is
covered in animals,

a smear of bacteria left from fingerprints, breath, other unnameable
residues

crushed together into what turns out to be a kind of signature

left behind on keyboards, buttons of the remote control, even in
the air of a room,

an aura of signatures

belonging to a person, lingering, bearing their name

through the air, puffed like a voice over the loudspeaker,

Laura, please come to the desk.

I always confuse *-trophic* with *-tropic*, to turn,

as in *heliotropic*, turning toward, the tendency of an animal to
move toward light

or *heliotrophic*, which must mean some sort of eating of the light,
but isn't a word at all, no matter how much I want it.

And it's like if I turn deep enough toward the static, which isn't
static but full of movement, laughter, noise,

I can step right into it, walk down it like a hall to the cafeteria, take
a little break,

and once I settle, I fold open the edges of the carton of vitamin D
milk and pour the white like light

over the table, carefully, obliterating every surface of the laminate,
letting gravity pull it toward the edges like a mother making a bed,
and I pour slowly, deliberately, until a kid shouts *hey!* and the nurse
comes over and grabs my wrist and pulls against gravity, up, up,
and twists me out of my chair and out of the

—light is itself a kind of turning toward before

its pixilation becomes too fine for the brain, finer than snow,
invisible but obvious as perfume, days later rumpled into the air
from a pillowcase, when it hits the piriform cortex

with its suspicion, small flicker

as when a lime tree shifts its leaves to eat the light

of aldehydes, something no mother ever wore, carrion flower
pulsing through the room like a throat, blood just below the skin

of an exhalation, and there's no one there after all but myself

of bergamot, civet, heliotrope.

Forest Floor

On waking after surgery for miscarriage

I've wanted to become more forest-like.
That is, to stretch toward blankness,

a sheet pulled too tight at the corners
of the twin mattress.

Everything is thin, thinned out,
I'd say threadbare, and even the air

I wrap around me like a quilt
feels cheap and doesn't warm up.

All afternoon eiderdown has been falling,
here, as I walk the O horizon,

unplucking itself from the skin
of the forest floor, sticking to my arms,

little pieces of down so soft
they don't seem to have any quill at all

until they prick, sudden pricking
over my skin, infinitesimal nibs

burrowing back into their goosebumps
and deeper into the follicle

toward muscle, burrowing
like earthworkers through mulch,

through flexors and extensors
inside me, brachialis, subclavius,

reaching toward lung as if wanting
in their burrowing to root

deep enough to reach air again,
to surface somewhere new

and not their own, in a body
in the middle of a breath

to fill my lungs with feathers
to make them buoyant, bloating

on the edgeless skin of a pond,
a severed wing I can't cough up,

and I try to explain to the nurse
when she places her hand on my head

and says some disorientation is normal,
and her face looks almost familiar,

a quilt handed down
from someone else's grandmother

tucked under my chin on a cold night,
and inside it I'm only one

invertebrate tuft, small as an oocyte,
nearly weightless, poreless,

all surface, unfilled with the impulse
to touch my own arms

to smooth the skin, as if I know
the feeling will pass, just a chill.

Common Fraction

Woke up like a nerve.
Air in the room is still
asleep, there and not there,
tacky wreck instead of touch.
Wall clock says five
and the afternoon nurse,
same nurse who
placed a mask over my face,
says something unconditional
and anesthetic, a hush
in the voice she used to say
deep breaths until the hiss, cold
as love, slipped a glove
over never and unselved me
like a sum. I put on my cloak
of blood and fur, hung
on the hook. I miss the *blank*
before it contracts like a cramp
inside a boot. The room
cleaves to my skin.
It has to be the air asleep,
since I'm here, awake.
What are your symptoms? I'm
asked. I'm not wearing boots.
I've forgotten some facts
about myself, such as how easy it is

to divide one into one.
How easy to deny that one
is divided, since one remains.
I'm in no condition to say.
Condition, from Latin, agreement:
con- (with) and *dicere* (say).
No, nothing came out of me.
Maybe I still have the one
lingering under my skirt.
Good grief. Who could say that?
Good died in my bed. I never agreed
to be myself, IV taped over
a single needle solved into a vein.

Mirror Stage

Glass of a thousand sands.
Glass that lets us see right through it.
I never wanted that kind of melting.
3200 degrees, sunlike, thin,
a sudden rooting inward.
You never get to come back
from that system.
I wanted to be terrestrial,
yielding as a handful
of sand—colorless brain an abacus.
It should be easy, not losing count.
It should be easy to say
without knowing the implications
the word *sand*, singular

     *

and then the dreams come,
silica slick in the bed afterward,
a whole world crushed like a pill
and melted, clear as a spinal
before my body hums home
its cells, turning me
into something countable,
mineral, a kind of currency
running down the river
behind my house, and I can sift
the sand with my fingers
until there's nothing left,
feeling the grains as they fall away
the tighter I make a fist.

Decomposition

Reproach, nowhere. Face of the clock
counts to three like a mother. Slowly,

cells knit new cells deep in the hardware
before REM cycles down.

There is no reason to startle awake.
Look, I ask myself, because I'm awake.

I'm ripping the seams out of a pair of jeans.
The pockets come off, a little blue,

with pilled cotton in the edges. It's something
to do, to skin a system to its mesoderm.

Just saying hi like a body is something
I've forgotten. It feels good,

like a hypercube, to hold the unfolded pattern
of my own legs, compliant in my lap.

*

Look. I'm a visitor here. The clock
isn't a mother and won't stop me

from placing on the table the lowball glass
cut with my initials I inherited

to prevent it from leaving its wet white ring
on the wood. The clock keeps counting

past three and doesn't stop or even startle
when I slip my hands into a knot

to stop myself threading through the fabric
the night has draped like a face

over my face, to hold it, and the clock
folds its hands but isn't a mother

no matter how much I want to hear her
tell me it's not too late to stop—

  *

—and her hands like needles sew little loops
in the shroud of space-time that I

have tried to take apart for so long, years,
pulling where the seams are permeable

as a dream, and for a moment it's dismantled
in the fabric on my lap, just a pair of jeans

that don't fit, nothing mysterious or individual
spliced into the cloth, and I don't have to look

to know how late it is when the clock begins
to wring its hands as if someone were expected,

circling without touching an interstitial center,
something unoiled, separate as a child,

fretting it until it's better to stay up,
resigned in orbit, until morning.

Waiting Room

Mother, fibrous mass in a lung, be sweeter to me, please.

When you call me from the hospital, don't do it with morphine in your mouth. Mother, please. I didn't know

when I was driving down one of those unnamed two-lane highways, the kind that starts at the border and ends in trompe l'oeil and the red cliffs, striated as a muscle, with the sun epicardial on the rock of the predictable west, somewhere out in the ass of Idaho with the cell signal on again off again and no gas station in recent memory

and the calls came in vibrating urgent and automatic in the cupholder and there was nowhere to pull over so I didn't answer the first time or the second and when I did pull over and called back there was no answer

and I drove some more—I don't even remember where I was going—some Sunday visit to the sublime, yellow grasses easier than church, and the bloodshot majesty

of a whole life hurtling toward a destination inside something like a Volvo, cradled in assurances of safety and the abstraction of speed, so it doesn't matter that I didn't get the voicemails until later and I'm already in the waiting room and the voice on the sequence of recordings gets steadily and noticeably more frantic, pitching toward panic,

accelerating out of the curve like my brother taught me, being older, reckless

toward a nothingness that could have been romantic and is suddenly absolute and terrible and real and small as the space inside a plastic chair molded to fit a body

that I can't fall asleep in under fluorescent lights, and I'm waiting to hear when or what or anything I don't know, waiting for the diagnosis

to change. I didn't know there is no cure for recovery, no destination outside of itself, no fire escape to step out onto to light your cigarette. It's something you're always in, living in like a room with the ceiling painted black so you can't see the smoke stain it yellow

as the grasses of the flood plain slurring the side window,

yellow as bilirubin building up just below the skin in the endless recovering, which is to say endless failure to recover, yellow as wet linoleum

dazzling back under the exit sign by someone wringing all the pink out of the mop into a biohazard bag and it's always one more relapse will be enough to stop

the liver from trying to repair itself, scrubbing the blood until it's
gone.

I'm supposed to call someone, I think, in a time like this. Family.
Brother, sister, some other. Some authority, someone outside
myself, but instead time folds itself into a rubber band I keep
messing with in my pocket, taking it out and pulling my hair back
and twisting and letting go and slipping it back onto my wrist.

That's how I know time is really human, unpredictable how long
before it snaps and I fall asleep by not thinking

about all the things a doctor can say: *late stage, scarring, low
hemoglobin count*. Hep C, sepsis, half-life

of a bottle of Klonopin. Or say: it's like a car accident, preventable
but irreversible.

Inflammation, viral infection. It's a story about contamination, not
about getting clean.

The floor is still wet and it smells like bleach

when I dial voicemail and listen. Mother, please stop. We can't go
back. I don't know what to say.

All those times in the car, kids asleep but our brains already wiring
up to arrive.

Mother, are we there yet?

Mother, by the time I got there I didn't know

the average life span of a red blood cell like the rubber band
around my wrist

ends with breaking.

Hemoglobin sounds to me like a celebratory word, a gift, *globo*,
bright balloon that never breaks, tied to a string the nurse hands to
a child

whose face for a moment flutters in delight at the color red.

Living Room

Season of lysis and low sun.
Season of lies. I smoked
a pack of wolves. First frost
chronic father—lover
of leaving let me tell you
for later. Let me tell you.
Let me peel the months
off my tongue in a long
single hair from my throat
I have swallowed
to become my throat
from a strand of DNA
that will denature me.
First lie, first lay, first getaway—
marry me—I was thrilled
through with sickness,
hemorrhaging red sun
on my sheets and me inside
growing awkward
into my own cell, totipotent,
peopled with grief.
Who? I ask. Who
could do such a thing:
people me with the honeybee.
All the things I can touch.
People me with fur,

with frostbitten jaw, just
there, with *there, there.*
Tell me a story
because I cannot stand
my ganglion of silence.
I was peopled with wolves,
lover, leaving me
mandible, bandaged
blastula, hollow ball
full of all the field
running through me,
muzzled with earth
where I tore belly first
into the wound and made
its dead center, incisor
tucked in a nest of fur
matted and licked,
its bracelet of nerves
nucleic, the hollow soft
and asymptomatic as a scar.

Decomp Sonnets

First day target dose little strip tease
slow as a cavity. I've been so good,
so accepting, lately,

of myself like a brother: baby boy
dissolving like Alka-Seltzer,
bicarbonate tablets becoming his eyes

and his eyes emptied out,
drunk up, bored and sick.

Our spine is curved as a labyrinth:
single footpath we follow

then I'm gone, not object of
nerve or love, all blood

just platelet, listening
to someone say swallow.

*

Easy expression, to kill
the pain. Which after all I can't

even finger through latex
its aggregate spirit,

superorganismic, part craving
part haunting. I've been borderline

historical all day: nostos
living inside me like a house

I can't remember in color
but in the smell

of cedar inside a chest, mine,
cat's cheek, vodka bottle in a sock,

attic morning
sick with sun.

    *

I've accepted things: tablets, tubes of saline.
There's no going back
from the slow strum in the vein,
hospital already chthonic,

somewhere linear I can't get to.
Slick lick of the gutted moon a stop codon
out the back of the rearview,
me with cuffs on,

night blotto with vomit,
mothering me. Who said I couldn't hit
her back? There's nothing

to relieve me of. Go ahead, search. Feel deep
in my pockets for an answer
to articulate in me like an artificial hip.

Dura Mater

n. the tough outermost membrane enveloping
the brain and spinal cord

Mother: land soft
into the howl wolf-deep in hill.
What is this place?
This path, striate
cortex down which I trace
a lineage of milk
white nerves becoming
from their great trunk
a single nerve that arrives
fine as a scalpel at the heart.
Mother, machined
from lung. Mother, the wolf
has already eaten your liver,
breathing hard her lupine
loam. Mother, your brain
a meniscus of yolk, sun
thick from the window
in the attic you lost,
where you sit at the machine
stitching wool I'll grow
to wear. Lay out the pieces
of tissue: flank, hip, waist, chest,
and with your silver scissors
cut me out. I ate your body
from the inside out.
The woods that run

up the hill, pines pinned
in place by glass, turn
to look. Turn—run,
mother morphine, mother mine,
but your limbs lumber,
you slumber sublingual,
suckled with the stars' sick milk.
Mother on the table,
shorn of wool. Mother feral.
Neural footpath
on the monitor goes straight
into the hypodermic dark.

Decomp

Morning has its tongue
again on the hospital windows

my side of the building,
feeling the lines for fracture

to pick a lock, which is
what a tongue does, speaks open.

Chances for getting out are nil.
Whole body of the place just like me

in triage, assemblage, kin
within just visiting. Depending

on how you count, I'm only one
tenth or one trillionth myself,

more bacteria than bone, glass
so clean I'm almost gone.

Ecological Self

eco-, from *oikos*, house
'Earth Household' is closer to the mark.
—ARNE NAESS

I've been doing a lot of wanting lately.
Saying to myself: I want a fin.

A wing, something kin, sudden
and certain inside my body.

Not just a metaphor, for example.
Real sun to eat out of a glass.

In order for this to happen,
I must be permeable. Homeostatic.

Like a strong ale, I hibernated
and now I'm ready.

Somewhere, outside, a little fox runs
across a parking lot and jumps into a dumpster.

Fox is looking for a word, a snack.
I let him in. I say come in.

I say you are *fox*
but he just stares right through it.

I keep my grid tight. As a predator,
I understand it's rude to stare.

I will go home covered in flex
of blood. I mean flecks.

Sorry. Something comes in,
something else comes out.

I will go home and eat my meat
without looking at its eye.

When I say covered in,
that means a surface is involved

but I can't remember which.
Maybe it's all just one surface.

Since I've been mastering
the art of terraforming,

nouns can be especially challenging.
I have a name for you:

stasis in a vortex.
No such thing.

Meat of apple and milk,
meat of nut and mutton.

Some I
I am. In my head

one x stays rhymeless.
That's what I've been trying to say.

I think the fox was eating the glass
when I watched him from my window.

He picked it up with his hands
and drank it like a sun.

Open Field

After Behavioral Analysis

Briefly, mice were placed in glass.
Briefly consisted of two open arms filled with light.

At first to be a mouse was defined
as the shape of a mouse: a value

followed by a small edge of fear.
Cue absence. The only movements

were videotapes of smaller mice
recorded and scored with days

of paws following and testing the perimeter.
Room to room to room.

The mouse was defined as cage,
as entering another room.

Cue walls arranged in open arms, arms
first making and holding the edges of home.

One open arm, two open arms,
a number of open arms.

Differentiating between context and context
allows an extinction of fear.

After all, mice are blind.
The mouse was an inclusion in a Plexiglass box.

Water, floor, water, floor,
combined in a common sign, grip.

In the clear level high tone
of a thermistor probe.

Time was blinded and placed on the platform.
Mice were arms of gray light,

lubricated and immobile open cages.
Mice were the thoroughly cleaned maze,

the maze of was and were
and footshock on a platform.

Cue fear, when animals were taken singly.
Central electric maze of a last memory

total and necessary in its head
before the nearest baseline was closed out.

Difference is an internal depth,
an interval. Individually, at least,

each second was like a red pedestal
to keep the unconditioned light.

Swim this time to the end. "The procedure
lasted 12 min per mouse per day."

Symbiosis

Take the simile. *Like* tastes firm like a tongue
on my tongue when it collapses

body and language—or is it body
and body—in its hinge.

Which one is real? The muscle or the word
in my mouth. The question

is like a predator
tearing into a living throat

or like its eyetooth
already inside my neck, its soft pulp

pulsating under the enamel like a seed
sensing dampness to root down

to an adrenal gland nested in nerves
or like my nerves braiding up

from the seed, subliminal,
to the skull.

It's not rhetorical.
Violence is part of the syntax

of my body: two copies
of every chromosome

severing themselves
around a centromere. An egg.

It's like a game of telephone:
I got it wrong.

I'm a whole book
of mothers, already bound,

overwritten with little gestures, neurons,
typos, all encoded.

Like mine, a mouse's tongue
is hidden, crouched in the house cat's jaw

just before
she crushes herself like a mouth.

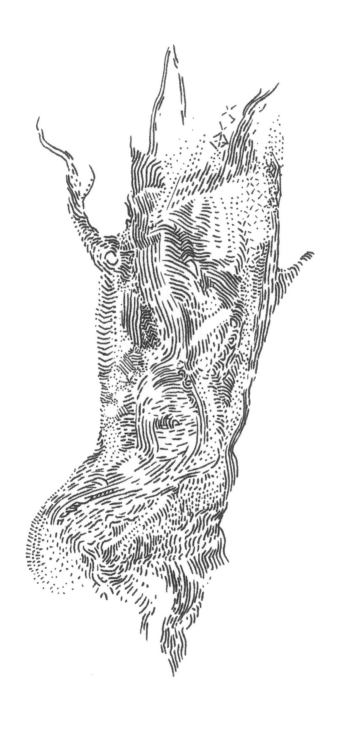

Autotheory

The problem
with saying the problem

is everything is
human is one of those

always already
theoretical conundrums.

The problem is everything
is funneled into language

before we even taste the air
is humid and the body is

swaddled to hide it from others.
Hide, noun, the skin

of an animal. Or *hide*, verb,
to keep out of sight,

as in the sentence: *the sacred relic
had been hidden away in a sealed cavern,*

with the dictionary's passive voice
hiding its subject,

perhaps just a kid still,
digging holes in the backyard

to stow away a colorful rock,
some coins, a time capsule,

childhood itself
not yet subterranean.

To hide it from others.
As if there were a self

contained by atmosphere
alone, and not

just the word *self* holding me
like a hand-knitted skin,

a nebula. As if from, say,
outer space, I could look

into a single eye
when I pluck up the planet

and hold it
by the scruff of its neck.

B73

genomic cartographers report an improved draft nucleotide
sequence of the 2.3-gigabase genome of maize

B73. Such a beautiful name. How do you say it? Oh, *Bee.*

*

My baby curls his toes, a reflex. At birth, there are four reflexes:
sucking, grasping, walking, and startle. With startle, the baby's
whole body reaches out and up and forward and toward the
mother like a seedpod, barbs out to grab at the nearby arm or
sweater, and even though he doesn't yet know he's terrified of
being dropped, his brain knows and directs the nerves and muscles
according to just such a terror. If you see the startle reflex, I'm told,
you should be more careful with your baby.

*

I say *he* because my baby is male assigned at birth. Or rather, male
assigned at NIPT, from a vial of my blood. At week twelve, when I
got the telephone call with the results from the genetic testing to
rule out XXX, the nurse said, "Do you want to know if it's a boy
or a girl?" with such delight—a secret—in the voice. As if without
the sex, the person isn't there: an it, object, not human, not yet.

*

And then there's the name. At first I tucked leaves from the little
vines of blue flowers growing wild in the lawn into the dictionary
of names to mark the letters, but then all the letters were marked.

I cut out petals from the pages. I gathered up names from all kinds of languages in a facsimile of violet, a collage, a vision for bees.

*

A name, you see, is a kind of power. A way of holding. I name you subject, shape. And it is heady, scented. A vial labeled in a cabinet of endless other names. When I hold you, I favor you like a sore muscle as I walk awkwardly down steps.

*

Power, unlike a reflex, must not be named. It is the act of naming that makes a subject. If I am not named, says the maize flower, I cannot be unnamed.

*

And a reflex doesn't have any real power, not yet. It's without conscious thought. Its power is only muscular, diagrammed, simple to understand.

*

I choose a purple crayon to draw my pain on the chiropractor's diagram. It's like a child's coloring book, with long muscles carefully outlined and shaded to indicate shape and strength. Iliacus, psoas, iliopsoas, adductor brevis, adductor longus, piriformis. Their names in Latin feel unfamiliar, which gives them power. But each muscle has a stretch. I can learn them, place ankle to knee and press to feel the pull.

*

As if calling pain not pain but by a name returns its power to my tongue like a thought, a word, and I can hold it there, contained. To my pain, I say I name you Bee and I make you your own.

*

I thought I knew every letter. Oh, Bee. Seedpods have a tough outer membrane, designed to split like the sky when it goes cornflower blue.

*

What a beautiful baby—what's his name?

Blue

The blanket is the first binary. Closed up, dressed in a signifier,
a baby becomes a metaphor. A sign. Easy as that. And when I
unwrap him I get to wiggle all of his *this little piggies*

teaching him to be vulnerable and invulnerable, covered in a name,
teaching everything has more than one direction. On and off, up
and down. It's not enough. Even to break it apart, a spectrum of
blue. Gravity is always there

to work against. We start at the top: *head, shoulders, knees, and
toes* and go back to tickling. I wave my open hand and say hello,
goodbye

in a single gesture. This is not a paradox. I want us to be
simultaneous, uncaged, tucked in a wing. When I say his name,
even as I speak I am

certain he is there and I am calling him, conjuring him from
absence, from where he never was,

not in the sky ripped-open blue that feels so close because it
scatters away, or in a star that disappears when I look directly at it,
just a function of biology, explainable by rods and cones, distance
and color, any time we look at something small or far away. Or
when we're standing at the edge of the lake

and I want to show him something, pointing to the ducks all the way across the surface with their hidden speculum of blue, and he follows the gesture, a sign, to something he can't see, and there I am with my body knitting all around me and I am only a moment

of waiting for someone to tuck something soft around my own shoulders, since the morning is full of cobalt and cold enough to see our breath.

Language Game

That I can speak
can't change certain facts.

The name *S typhi*, derived
from the ancient Greek *typhos*,

comes from an ethereal smoke or cloud
believed to cause disease and madness.

Salmonella typhi look a little like Mike and Ike's.
I carry with me this capacity for metaphor,

even when it seems absurd
or maybe especially then. In this moment,

is it absurd (*surdus*, sordo, hard to hear, off tune)
to bring myself a plate of candy?

After all, sugar is so sweet
I can't hear anything it says.

Zea mays

Maize kernel like a gold tooth
lodges its symbol in my mouth:

of power, two-pronged, unpurchasable
as lineage, ironic as a question:

who wouldn't allow herself to die
like the nerve in a tooth to place a name:

bicuspid crown, on her child's head,
ten-thousandth grandchild of the wild grass:

before selling it to a stranger,
a kernel to take home and make into a house:

sort of like in "Jack and the Beanstalk"
in which the beanstalk deep in Jack's pocket:

calls to his fingers and carefully Jack
fingers the seeds he has purchased:

listening, and he places them under the soil
of his tongue to learn their speech:

of lions barking and pulling at a leash of vine
against the wishes of their mother:

their wanting growing upward
against the gravity of time:

toward some wildness, matted
as dead roots but still carried, coiled inside:

lost feral firstborn kept like a scar
imprinted in the chaff:

in the halo of mane I pull back
so casually to check for rot:

none of my tendrils listening
to their tongues ruddy and lolling:

over yellow and white incisors
like butter and sugar corn cobs:

salivating and muscular tongues
naming their price:

Oogenesis

In the kind of story I want to tell,
the coin can only ever be a metaphor.

The predators need something to eat.
Flightless firstborn, ungerminated,

small and empty as a needle's eye,
will have to do.

Mothers carry their daughters
with their own daughters already in them,

millions of the littlest eggs bursting forth
like popcorn out of nothing

at twenty weeks, in a body barely bigger
than the egg I cooked for breakfast.

Some of them must zero out.
As if that were a consolation,

some sewn into sheets, clean cotton
and just a thread of blood,

a generation of proof,
then poof—rich in protein and fat,

a major source of vitamins
and the minerals Ca, Fe, P, K, Zn,

full spectrum of B,
on sale a dozen for ninety-nine cents

and I rock each one gently
to check it's not broken

before I pay the cashier
and carry them out in their Styrofoam nest.

Model Organism

Hunt her not
in thought: taut scar
-let tissue torn
from other, elsewhere
hold her

reach your hand into the comb
and pull it back
honeyed, married

*

It is not a question
I can ask
whether the bees
can abstract

a small symbol, *a*

petite
as a first arrest

cardiac then respiratory
then legs wrangled Qter/Pter

*

My incisor: Little *melissa*,

my sister
softer terminal

  *

they can fold my
glasses up,
cut a piece of me off.

We are moving as one,
wrecked

grass tracked on the carpet

rill of muscle will
writhe
to hold me
my other, my daughter cells

diligent, as if
they could keep anything out
by building each her very own wall

Living Room

On the hypothetical origin of eukaryotic cells

House of membranes
and mice in the walls.

House of rupture
draped like a dress

sliced from the neck
to hip, DNA unzippering

on the brick caked with lime.
I might let just anyone in

for the talk and then to stay
to feel the afternoon,

a slow vine's leash of forest
in synthesis, climbing

and in turns trailing,
wrapping itself over the wall,

hugging the body, a leg,
tree as it stretches toward sun.

*

I'm telling myself things
as if everything is relational:

when I say *is*, I mean juxtaposition
not definition. Like a stranger,

the leash grows curious and reaches
with its fringed fingers,

feeling around for warmth,
more sun, softness in the light,

the same synesthesia of touch and taste
my tongue has always known,

feeling the full cream of air
firm as arms wrapped around my chest

and the whole house filled
to the roof of its mouth

with the fine mist of morning
on a lake of air and milk

    *

I'm moving through
from room to room, following

my visitors, attentively, to stack
their cups and plates like stones

in the wake of our path
in an infinite conversation

of walls. I cup the stone I am
holding to my mouth,

close enough to be continuous,
tucked in a broom closet,

and where the room is enclosed
inside another inside

is outside again, where
I'm growing in a skin of cells,

intrinsic as sun
sudden on the lichen.

    *

I think I've never been alone
in the room I'm living in,

or is it the living room
I've been for years,

together with others
for longer than I've been alive

in a chamber of dry stone
with two faces in a single wall,

a cell sweet as a comb
where a guest or a prisoner

or I might sleep into the afternoon,
dreaming of the way light

tastes first crustlike, carbon,
then honey in a holding in

by my own slow-growing arms
of lungwort, dog-pelt, sunburst.

Habit

In oxidation-reduction, electrons transfer
from one species to another.

Take, for example, toothpaste. "We knew
that fluoride is taken up into the tooth,"

says the crystallographer. "But there was no proof
of where it was actually going."

Here, one species is sodium
and one species is human.

Without realizing, I've been holding
my electrons, fingering them like coins.

When the crystallographer goes home
somewhere in the evening,

she teaches her child to brush his teeth
without thinking about the toothpaste.

The key is to do it so many times,
it becomes automatic.

Automatic, via Latin: acting of itself.
Here, *it* is an act that will live

inside the boy and inhabit him
for good. A good habit.

And the self, which is an act
inside the boy, will dream

in tendrils he doesn't need to listen to
to understand what they say.

Spit, the crystallographer says, and he does.
We know that language is taken up

like fluoride, but we don't know
where it goes. In a few years,

the boy will lose his first tooth
and hold it tight in his small palm

until deep in the pillowspace, a nerve
comes forth from the kernel and grows.

Heirloom

Jack hid some money in his bedpost and didn't tell anyone that it was there, not even his friend Cha-cha-cha.

*

Jack left the money in the bedpost for so long that it was no longer money, just an old portrait.

*

He thought about it every night as he drifted off to sleep in his blanket. On one side of the portrait was a pastoral scene etched with grasses and a milkless cow and every night Jack walked the same path he always walked and fingered the grasses heavy with seed.

*

In the finger's depth topsoil of his dream, Jack hid the seeds he purchased (*from whom?—providence was the real agent here, not the old vendor, fraying fur around her face, skin pulled thin and gray as an unused udder, starched ruff, kin to no one and gone when Jack returned to try to undo the bargain*).

*

Cha-cha-cha was a small and long-furred cow, with a mane that went ember in the sun and petite hooves soft as the palm of Jack's hand. Every morning Jack woke up in the still dark to milk her and scratch her ears and sing to her the filaments of his dream.

*

For many years, Jack walked the stalls of the market looking for the one who gave him the dream, but she had hidden herself in the long white hair of the grass.

*

Hide, verb, to conceal from the notice of others. On Saturdays, Jack would dig up the backyard with his gardening spade, overturning the surface. He would watch squirrels sift for acorns. The skin around his eyes darkened and thickened to hide.

*

Cha-cha-cha grew smaller and smaller with the years, thinning up, her milk almost water, then water, before it was gone.

*

Jack began to drink only water. He drank water every morning and every night but nothing could help his thirst. He carried water in a leather flask out to the yard and took a drink and poured the last of it over his face.

*

He began to count the same things twice. Sunrises were yesterday's and today's since he didn't sleep. Steps from his room to the door and back. He was never alone in his head. Maybe he was the giant all along, he said.

*

Jack followed the grass to the edge of the yard but the edge disappeared. *Setaria viridis*, just common grass. Common, as in it filled him with community. Gave him family and order. It grew so much more than up, rooting itself like a castle into the air.

*

Cattle, capital, and captain all have the same Latin root, *caput*, meaning head, not related to *kaput*, meaning broken, worthless.

*

Nobody came to steal from him. He locked his door every night and he waited and every night ended. There was no legend in the map of sun on the curtain. No dreams, no face to search for wrapped in fur. All he had was a hoof, two-chambered like a heart, and he pressed it into the earth. When he stepped out of his body, Jack's skin curled into an old dollar bill, hidden in his room.

*

A boy arrived to sweep and open the windows and throw out the sheets, but grass filled every corner of the house.

Fairy Tale with Redox

There is a room I'm thinking of in a rustic cabin, one I might have visited in a dream, abandoned and locked, but with a lock easy to pick, big splintered wooden planks and a dead bolt like a tongue, oxidation all over it, the slow reaction of oxygen and iron exchanging electrons.

*

Iron searches the market stalls, looking in face after face of each merchant, asking for their price, feeling the electron hot in the palm of his hand, burning straight through, ready, and he's ready to buy something, anything, to fill his belly that isn't milk.

*

This is one way to describe it:
$$2Fe \rightarrow 2Fe^{2+} + 4e\text{-}$$

*

The boy gives the vendor his milk cow.

*

The iron ion and the hydroxide ion react to form iron hydroxide:
$$2Fe^{2+} + 4OH^- \rightarrow 2Fe(OH)_2$$

*

The cow realizes she is leaving her house. She is free. She is expelled. She is gone.

*

And once she's gone from the story, that's it. Who knows what happens. I don't want a rhetorical question. Red as what. Subconjunctival hemorrhage. Hook through the feet like socks of blood. I can't say it because there is no need. After all, without being told so in a fairy tale, children know that robbery and murder are wrong. The cow ate sweet grass until she went to sleep.

Elegy with Redox

I placed some coins in a box
and I buried it and I
told myself not to forget
exactly where and exactly
where this occurred
I marked with a stone.
And exactly where
this occurred I knew
knowledge of a purely
corporeal nature in its
relation of time : space
and time : space held
the box and the air and coins
and the air made of O
[oxygen, exclamation, an open mouth]
began to wrap its mouth
around the coins and suck,
tonguing them tucked
under the roof, sucking
[which is an act of drawing into
the mouth for nourishment]
and sucking *[which is a reflex]*
on lemonhead candy

[*C12/H22/O11*] and the air
ate the coins and the coins
disappeared into the soil
[this is called oxidation]
in a spot of rust *[reduction]*
like blood on a sock
I can't pick out.

Redox

I've been feeling mitochondrial.
After all, a cell is also a room

with organs, furniture, pictures on the wall.
Light comes in like a handful of neurotransmitters

kept deep in my pocket of brain.
I've been keeping things shallow.

Hello. Let me wreck good morning
before I wreck the rest. Keeping things

in the right order is one way.
Let me place a berry on my tongue.

Last night rusted like a damaged hinge
and now there's no way out.

Recall: oxidation is an act of stealing.
Cell wall can't stop iron, ferrum.

Nothing is fair. Don't think I won't
set fire to the house. Daybreak

feels literal in my chest, almost
human, sliced like fruit on a plate.

Let me taste how sweet
burns easiest all the way to carbon.

Parable of the Wolf

Nothing on us but days
measured like contractions.
Count down from ten
and pull wool from my
skin in wet tufts.
At the river, trees
hold fruit up to the sun
as if to inspect
a glass after washing.
Skin translucent.
In Aesop, certain
unlikeliness arises
between wolf and the word
wolf that fits in a mouth
as if the mouth were
a lamb—a wolf, not
always unlike
her own pink tongue
lapping at a small pool
before she lifts
her head to say *come out*.
Little one, don't come out.
Stay in my ventricle

whole, ectopic.
She lifts her head
to tell me with my tongue
where she has been hiding,
thoracic, lunglike
inside me all along
and how to grip the nape
and split the body
so her spine comes out
like a root letting go
of the dirt.

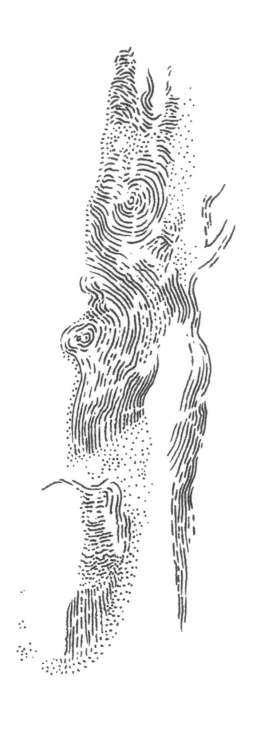

NOTES

"Ecological Self": Arne Naess introduced the term "ecological self" in his writings on deep ecology to account for our identification with nonhuman living beings and our immediate environment as fundamental constitutive relationships. The epigraph is taken from his book *Ecology, Community and Lifestyle* (Cambridge University Press, 1990).

"Open Field": The source text for this poem comes from the supporting information section of Javier A. Bravo et al., "Ingestion of Lactobacillus Strain Regulates Emotional Behavior and Central GABA Receptor Expression in a Mouse via the Vagus Nerve," *PNAS* 108, no. 38 (2011): 16050–55. The section in question describes testing procedures in a study in mice (*Mus musculus*) on the effects of administered probiotics. All words in the poem are taken from the section and used, unaltered, exactly once.

"B73": B73 is the variant of maize (*Zea mays*) first chosen by the scientific community to have its genome sequenced. The epigraph is taken from Patrick S. Schnable et al., "The B73 Maize Genome: Complexity, Diversity, and Dynamics," *Science* 326 (2009): 1112–15.

"Model Organism": Model organisms are nonhuman species studied and sequenced to understand specific biological phenomena, and they include viruses, prokaryotes, and eukaryotes such as protists, fungi, plants, and animals. Common plant and animal models include maize (*Zea mays*), the chicken (*Gallus gallus domesticus*), the mouse (*Mus musculus*), and the honeybee (*Apis mellifera*), among many others.

"Living Room" [House of membranes]: The subtitle is taken from a section title in Lynn Margulis's 1967 paper, "On the Origin of Mitosing

Cells," which posits what is now known as the endosymbiotic theory, the leading evolutionary theory of the origin of eukaryotic cells from prokaryotic organisms through the process of symbiosis. Lungwort, dog-pelt, and sunburst are lichens. Notable here is that lichens are not plants; they are complex lifeforms composed of algae and fungi living in a symbiotic partnership, in which the fungal partner provides the structure but cannot produce its own food, and the algal partner provides food from sunlight through photosynthesis.

"Habit": "We knew that fluoride is taken up . . ." is quoted from Mark Peplow, "How Fluoride Firms up Teeth," *Nature*, (2004), https://doi.org/10.1038/news040119-8.

"Heirloom": *Setaria viridis* is a hardy species of grass, also a model organism, commonly found growing in urban and disturbed habitats such as sidewalks or vacant lots.

ACKNOWLEDGMENTS

I offer my many thanks to the journals in which these poems originally appeared, sometimes under different titles or in earlier forms:

Arts & Letters: "Autotheory" and "Dura Mater"
Crazyhorse: "Decomp Sonnets"
DIAGRAM: "Waiting Room," "Waiting Room," and "Open Field"
The Journal: "Mirror Stage" and "Decomposition"
Juked: "Autotheory"
PANK: "Redox" and "Blue"
RHINO: "Decomp"
The Spectacle: "Parable of the Wolf," "Ecological Self," and "Model Organism"
Vinyl: "Living Room"

Thank you to Huascar Medina for selecting the manuscript, and to everyone at the University of Nebraska Press for your care in bringing it into the world.

Thank you to the University of Mary Washington for support through a faculty research grant and a Jepson fellowship. Also to my department, colleagues, and students for helping me root myself in the forests of Virginia.

Endless thanks and love to my fellows and friends for reading and rereading, for the conversations, the closeness and distance, and for the taproots of old friendships, especially to Claire Wahmanholm, Cass Donish, Sara Eliza Johnson, Susannah Nevison, Ray Levy, Thomas

Bechtold, Lauren Reding, Nathie Katzoff, Melissa Braxton, Sarah Sarchin, and Jezebel St. John.

Thank you to my family, to my mother for always listening, and to my father for showing me how to see closely. Thank you to my brother for sharing his uncommon strength and insight. And thank you to Israel and Leon for giving me their perfect light. This book is for them.

BACKWATERS PRIZE IN POETRY

2021   Laura Bylenok, *Living Room*
       Honorable Mention: Sophie Klahr, *Two Open Doors in a Field*
2020   Nathaniel Perry, *Long Rules: An Essay in Verse*
       Honorable Mention: Amy Haddad, *An Otherwise Healthy Woman*
2019   Jennifer K. Sweeney, *Foxlogic, Fireweed*
       Honorable Mention: Indigo Moor, *Everybody's Jonesin' for Something*
2018   John Sibley Williams, *Skin Memory*
2017   Benjamín Naka-Hasebe Kingsley, *Not Your Mama's Melting Pot*
2016   Mary Jo Thompson, *Stunt Heart*
2015   Kim Garcia, *DRONE*
2014   Katharine Whitcomb, *The Daughter's Almanac*
2013   Zeina Hashem Beck, *To Live in Autumn*
2012   Susan Elbe, *The Map of What Happened*
2004   Aaron Anstett, *No Accident*
2003   Michelle Gillett, *Blinding the Goldfinches*
2002   Ginny MacKenzie, *Skipstone*
2001   Susan Firer, *The Laugh We Make When We Fall*
2000   David Staudt, *The Gifts and the Thefts*
1999   Sally Allen McNall, *Rescue*
1998   Kevin Griffith, *Paradise Refunded*

The Backwaters Prize in Poetry was suspended from 2005 to 2011.

To order or obtain more information on these or other University of
Nebraska Press titles, visit nebraskapress.unl.edu.

Lightning Source UK Ltd.
Milton Keynes UK
UKHW010903180822
407484UK00001B/126